THE ROMANS CAME THIS WAY

THE STORY OF THE DISCOVERY AND EXCAVATION OF A ROMAN MILITARY WAY ACROSS THE YORKSHIRE PENNINES

Norman Lunn
Bill Crosland
Bonwell Spence
Granville Clay

HUDDERSFIELD AND DISTRICT ARCHAEOLOGICAL SOCIETY

Published by Huddersfield and District Archaeological Society.

ISBN : 978-0-905747-03-3

Designed by Scarlet Solutions, Bradford, Tel: 01274 818104

Printed in the UK by the Charlesworth Group
Flanshaw Way, Flanshaw Lane, Wakefield WF2 9LP

NORMAN LUNN

This book is dedicated to Norman Lunn who was a leading member of the Society almost from its formation in 1956.

It is largely due to his energy, enthusiasm and expertise as an amateur archaeologist that so much was accomplished in the search for the road.

No problem was too difficult for Norman to overcome, and his wisdom and good humour were an inspiration to those who had the privilege to work with him.

He was very much concerned with the preparation of this volume and the CD which accompanies it, but sadly in October 2007 he died without realising his wish to see the completed work.

It is very appropriate that his ashes were scattered at Pule Hill, a site which along with others in the Society he had come to view with some affection.

Plate 1 - Norman Lunn and the 'road of quality' for which he searched for more than 30 years.

FORERUNNERS

Authors and historians who helped to stimulate the search for the true course of the Roman road across the Pennine hills.

This Military way ... passes through Saddleworth by Marsden Chapell to Huddersfield.

JohnWarburton 1720, British Museum, Lansdowne MSS.

The Roman highway, tradition records, approaches Marsden village from the north-east ... eventually leaving Pule Hill to the right ...

L.B. Whitehead, *Bygone Marsden*, (Percy Brothers Ltd., Hotspur Press. 1942) p.48.

... [it] passes by the foot of Pule Hill, tending towards Marsden. But it can easily be connected with Slack by turning northward from Marsden by Slaithwaite-hall and Pole ...

Rev. D.H. Haigh, *YAJ*, Vol.4 (1877), p.56.

... from the eastern gate [Castleshaw] there is a broad, well-defined indication of a road up the moor, which crosses the farmlands at Brown Rough, climbs over the moor top and runs down behind the Great Western Inn.

Ammon Wrigley, *Songs of a Moorland Parish*, (1912) p.303.

CONTENTS

CD   The enclosed compact disc has additional information on some of the excavation sites as listed above, including reports, plans, section drawings and photographs. A full list of contents can be found on the CD.

PLATES

The route of the Roman road from Castleshaw fort in Saddleworth to Slack fort at Outlane, Huddersfield crosses private land or land owned by the National Trust. Those wishing to observe the route of the road, as illustrated in this book, can do so, in the main, from public roads and pathways close to the road. The National Trust Marsden Moor Estate is 'open access' but the terrain can be difficult and dangerous in places.

Evidence of the road on the surface is scarce, but it is a worthwhile exercise to follow the chosen route of the Roman surveyors as they took the road over the high moorland and through the steep contours of the Colne Valley.

Remember

Do not enter private land, which has no right of way, without the permission of the landowner.

Do not disturb soil or vegetation on, or near, the road.

Do not disturb or remove stones.

Do not remove artefacts or archaeological material found along the route.

ACKNOWLEDGEMENTS

The authors give grateful recognition to the very many who have contributed to this investigation, including the following:

Reports / Surveys
Arnold Aspinall
Nuala Moran
John Walker
Jane Wheeler
Emma Wood

Landowners & Farmers
Dartmouth Estates
National Trust
Brian Bamforth
Robert Bamforth
Jack Bramall
Julie & Gary Crawford
David Dodson
Mr & Mrs G. Dransfield
Peter Garside
Richard Garside
Lee Gilbert & Ian Dodds
Lynda & Richard Hayton
Mr & Mrs G. Pashley
Mr G. Walker

Diggers & Helpers
Sidney Akroyd
Darren Bailey
Geoff Baldwin
John Bowen
Warren Bower
Nick Brook
Alan Crosland
Alistair Crosland
Christine Crosland
W.B. Cornfoot
Brenda Dudley
Eric Eastwood
Stephen Frost
A.E. Hargreaves
Patrick Harte
Mary Hartland
J.M. Hickson
Frances Hobart
Barry Hobson
Geoff Holdsworth
Sue Horne
Brian Howcroft
Neda Howcroft
Gillian Hoyle
David Hynes
Russell Irving
Geoffrey Lunn
Liesel Lunn
Stephen Lunn
Stella Marks
Neil Marsay
George Monk
Olive Monk

Brian Moriarty
Bob Moss
Dorothy Moss
Martin Moss
Steven Nuttall
Chris O'Prey
Mark Pennington
Fiona Phelan
Jean Thornes
Peter Thornes
Edward Vickerman
Gary Ward
Irene Watkins
Pat Woods
Philip Woods
Steven Wroe

Site Visitors
David Clarke
David Finnis
Margaret Freeman
Mary Freeman
John Hedges
Rick Jones
Jenny Keighley (Marriott)
Phillip Mayes
Doug Moir
Mark Newman
Norman Redhead
Dave Start
John Walker
Bob Yarwood

Special thanks to Dr Rob Vernon and Edward Vickerman for their help and advice in preparing this publication.

FOREWORD

I first came across the work of the Huddersfield and District Archaeological Society when it was judged to be the runaway winner of the Mick Aston Presentation Award at the British Archaeological Awards ceremony in 2004. This award, which I am happy to sponsor, is for the 'best presentation of an archaeological project or theme to the public, thus stimulating awareness of, and curiosity about, our national heritage'.

As a passionate believer in making archaeology accessible to the general public, I shared the view of the judges that the Society's presentation of the 'Myers Wood Project', the exploration of a mediaeval iron making site, had been 'vigorous, professional, and widely praised'.

Not content to rest on its laurels the Society has now embarked on a public presentation of a remarkable piece of archaeological research that has spanned more than thirty years and is still continuing. This book tells the fascinating story of how a dedicated group of amateur archaeologists found themselves challenging all the accepted theories of where and how the Roman army built a major military road across the Pennines.

The results of the Society's efforts to demonstrate the continuous route of this previously unknown road are set out here in a well illustrated and readable narrative. For those wishing to dig deeper into the evidence, there are supporting excavation reports, drawings, plans and site photographs.

Research that leads to a better understanding of how the Romans influenced our present day towns, villages, roads and landscape, is to be welcomed. That this can be achieved by an active local archaeological society is clearly demonstrated in this publication.

Mick Aston

Emeritus Professor of Archaeology at Bristol University and

Archaeological Consultant to Channel 4's 'Time Team'

INTRODUCTION

The road linking the legionary bases at Chester and York passes by the forts at Castleshaw on the Lancashire side of the Pennines before crossing the high moorland to Slack, near the village of Outlane, on the Yorkshire side. From the late first century this was a route of paramount strategic importance to the Roman army as it moved northwards in its conquest of Britain.

From Manchester to Castleshaw the line has been well established[1] but that from Slack to Tadcaster is very much open to conjecture. The line from Castleshaw to Slack a distance of 12 kilometres (7.5 miles) over difficult country has been the subject of much speculation but very little positive identification. Since its formation in 1956 the Huddersfield Society has pursued possible routes as part of a continuous programme of fieldwork. It was however in reality a chance discovery in 1973 which provided the first clue as to where we should be looking.

This publication then includes descriptions of a series of excavations. The conclusions derived from these investigations support the line of a road between Castleshaw and Slack which is almost complete.

Here it is perhaps appropriate to pause a moment in order to give a very brief outline of the Society's background and hence its experience in fieldwork and excavation: a sort of abridged Curriculum Vitae.

From the first, Roman interest took it to Grimscar to excavate the tile kilns.[2] Then to Slack to assist Kay and Brian Hartley in their work both on the fort and the *vicus*, and then back to the *vicus* again on its own account. Jim Toomey directed excavation on the Iron Age sites at Oldfield Hill[3] and Royd Edge, Meltham,[4] finding no evidence to support assertions that the former had Roman connections. Bonwell Spence and Stella Marks worked on the moated house at South Crosland Hall, and Norman Lunn spent a number of seasons excavating and surveying the cairns and other features at Hagg Wood[5] and Slate Pits Wood, Meltham.[6] Members were very much involved with Dr. W. J. Varley at Castle Hill, Almondbury; and in Calderdale Norman Lunn and Bill Crosland investigated the Meg Dyke enclosure at Barkisland. Prior to 1973 the Society had excavated only one section of Roman road[7] that being on Lindley Moor two kilometres east of the Slack fort.

Many other minor projects could be noted, but mention must be made of the Society's involvement, from 2001 onwards, in the award winning Myers Wood project,[8] the investigation of a mediaeval iron working site, researched in tandem with the University of Bradford. In the summer of 2007 the Society returned to the *vicus* at Slack where a number of important discoveries were made, and research on the Roman road was resumed.

The forts at Castleshaw and Slack have common construction dates of around AD 79. Current knowledge indicates that Castleshaw[9] was abandoned in perhaps AD 120 when a withdrawal was necessitated by the requirement to build and garrison Hadrian's Wall. Excavation evidence suggested that Slack was occupied for a further 20 years and it was assumed that closure in AD 140 was contemporary with the construction of the Antonine

Wall.[10] Almost certainly after AD 140 there was little need to provide a large military presence in this sparsely populated area of Brigantia, although occupation continued at Manchester[11] into the fourth century. It was thought that the road, no longer being of any military importance, would gradually go out of use and maintenance would cease. However, evidence from the 2007 Society excavations at Slack, including radiocarbon dating and pottery finds, suggests that the site was active long after the supposed military withdrawal, with the possibility that the road continued to be used as a major transpennine route throughout the second century and even later.

From Castleshaw fort, the way to Slack passes through fields to the farm at Brown Rough where it turns to make the ascent of Standedge; it can be seen on the ground and more clearly in aerial photographs. At this point however certainty stops, to be overtaken by speculation.

Thomas Percival who together with the Rev. John Watson discovered the Castleshaw fort wrote in 1751 :-

> *'From Castleshaw the Roman way goes directly for the hill called Clowze-moss, where it was cut thro' the moss, and is called Old Gate, being visible by the greeness of its tract, so over the top of Clows or Clowze-moss. It is visible in a green tract over the Reaps (a hill so called) leaving March-hill or Marshill a little to the north and Marsden about a mile and a half to the south, pointing directly on Pole-moor, going in its way over the middle of Holm-moor, and so directly up Cupwith-moor to Pole moor stone, or Guide post above Slaighwait or Glaighwait and along the north of Gowkerhill or Wholestone moor, or Hoolstone moor, leaving the rocking-stone about 500 yards to the south.'*

It thus became generally accepted that the nature of Close Moss which abounds with steep cloughs and peat bogs would prevent any crossing, and that the route would turn north along what is now the Standedge section of the Pennine Way as far as Oldgate Clough. Here it descends towards March Haigh reservoir. W.B. Crump writing in his 'Huddersfield Highways Down the Ages'[12] explains the difficulty of the hollow at March Haigh under the Buckstones, but continues to say that on reaching the line of New Hey Road, somewhere near to Worts Hill, all was easy.

This line from March Hill to Slack was almost universally accepted particularly as Margary[13] reinforces this view. He considers that from Castleshaw the road climbs to March Hill and thereafter it could be represented by the present A640 Oldham to Huddersfield road which runs in straight lengths as far as Pole Moor. The difficulty of course was that in spite of the efforts of many people on both sides of the Pennines there was no convincing evidence of a road anywhere along this route.

In 1968, in advance of the construction of the M62 motorway, Brian Hartley[14] of the University of Leeds excavated in the *vicus* of Slack fort. He clearly demonstrated the Chester to York road running almost due west to east and traversing the *vicus* some 100 metres from the north gate of the fort. At that time with the eye of the believer it was possible to identify a continuing line passing through neighbouring fields for perhaps 200 metres. However any such road, present and intact at that time, was almost certainly destroyed by the motorway contractors.

Members of the Society had been very much involved in walking, surveying and studying the favoured route from Slack; but at the same time keeping other options open. Particular interest was taken in Worts Hill and its environs and the possibility of a signal station on Wholestone Moor was never ruled out. As well as they were able they kept a close watch on the preparatory work for the M62, but nothing was seen which would indicate a road. There was in fact very little to show for the effort involved and the many hours of fieldwork.

Only one very remote possibility of a line west of the fort emerged. Waterworn cobbles perhaps from a road surface were present on the steep ascent of the path to Wholestone Moor which leaves Round Ings Road near to the farm of that name. The gradient would however seem to render this route impractical if better alternatives were available.

All this negative evidence does not mean that the Standedge, Oldgate Clough, Worts Hill road doesn't exist; nevertheless the best efforts of this Society have failed to find it. Looked at from the perspective of both the Roman engineers and the legions who were to use it, in reality this is not a good route; it is by no means the best Pennine crossing. Winter here can be both long and severe; therefore it makes good sense to avoid high altitude if at all possible. If the nature of the terrain dictates that excessive elevation cannot be avoided then there are obvious advantages in minimizing the distance to be travelled at an uncomfortable height. Standedge is almost 450 metres above sea level and is extremely exposed to the prevailing winds. The 'Percival route' would have to maintain this height along the ridge for at least two kilometres before attempting the steep and boggy descents and ascents associated with March Haigh Clough.

This was the position and sum of knowledge in the autumn of 1973 when the Society was invited to have a look at a feature in a field near to a causeway at Moorside Edge, Slaithwaite, overlooking the Colne Valley. It was the discoveries made here which stimulated the further research described in this volume and which has made it possible to plot the unexpected route of the road. The following chapters will show how this became an ever changing story and even as the book was being written, new and important discoveries were being made.

It has been decided to present the digs in chronological order rather than as a topographical sequence. This may well make it difficult for the reader who wishes to follow the route on the ground, but we submit that it allows a presentation which is both logical in its content and interesting as a story.

It is perhaps useful here to add a short footnote on the builders of the road, for after all they were the recipients of toasts drunk at dig suppers associated with the excavations. The Roman army took its communications very seriously and there is much evidence to tell us that when not engaged on purely military or policing duties, road building would be a high priority. Tiles made at the Grimscar kiln are found at both Slack[15] and Castleshaw;[16] they bear the stamp COHIIIIBRE, the 4th cohort of Breuci. This unit is presumed to be the garrison of at least one of the forts and consequently the principal road builder in our area of interest. It was one of a series of eight cohorts raised from the Breuci in Pannonia;[17] it probably served in Germany before its transfer to Britain in perhaps AD 43. Under Julius Severus (130-133) it is attested as building at Bowes and in the third century it is at Ebchester.

REFERENCES

1. Haigh D. *A Survey of Roman Road Margary 712 Through The Oldham Area.*
    Bradford Grammar School Archaeological Society and The 712 Group (1982)

2. Hallam A. 'The Roman Tilery in Grimscar Wood'. *HDAS Bulletin* No.16. (1965)

3. Toomey J. P. 'An Iron Age enclosure at Oldfield Hill, Meltham'.
    Special report, *HDAS Brigantian* (1976)

4. Toomey J. P. 'An inner ditch enclosure at Royd Edge, Meltham'.
    HDAS Brigantian Vol. 5. (1982)

5. Lunn N. 'A preliminary report on the 1963 excavations at Hagg Wood'.
    HDAS Bulletin No.13. (1963)

6. Lunn N. *Slate Pits Wood, Meltham.* HDAS (2002)

7. Crosland W. E. 'A Roman Road at Lindley Moor'. *Brigantian* Vol. 1. (1972)

8. Clay G., McDonnell G., Spence B. and Vernon R.
    The Iron Makers of Myers Wood. HDAS Revised 2nd Edn. (2006)

9. Walker J. S. F. (ed.) *Castleshaw. The Archaeology of a Roman Fortlet.*
    Greater Manchester Archaeological Unit. (1989)

10. Dodd and Woodward. 'Excavations at Slack 1913-1915'.
    Journal of the Yorkshire Archaeological Society. (1922)

11. Walker J. S. F. (ed.). *Manchester. A Frontier Settlement.*
    Greater Manchester Archaeological Unit. (1986)

12. Crump W. B. *Huddersfield Highways Down The Ages.*
    The Tolson Memorial Museum. (Huddersfield, 1949)

13. Margary I. D. *Roman Roads in Britain.* (London, 1967)

14. Hartley and Fitts. *The Brigantes.* Alan Sutton. (1998)

15. Dodd and Woodward. 'Excavations at Slack 1913-1915'.
    Journal of the Yorkshire Archaeological Society. (1922)

16. Walker J. S. F. (ed.) *Castleshaw. The Archaeology of a Roman Fortlet.*
    Greater Manchester Archaeological Unit. (1989)

17. Holder P. A. *The Roman Army in Britain.* Batsford. (1982)

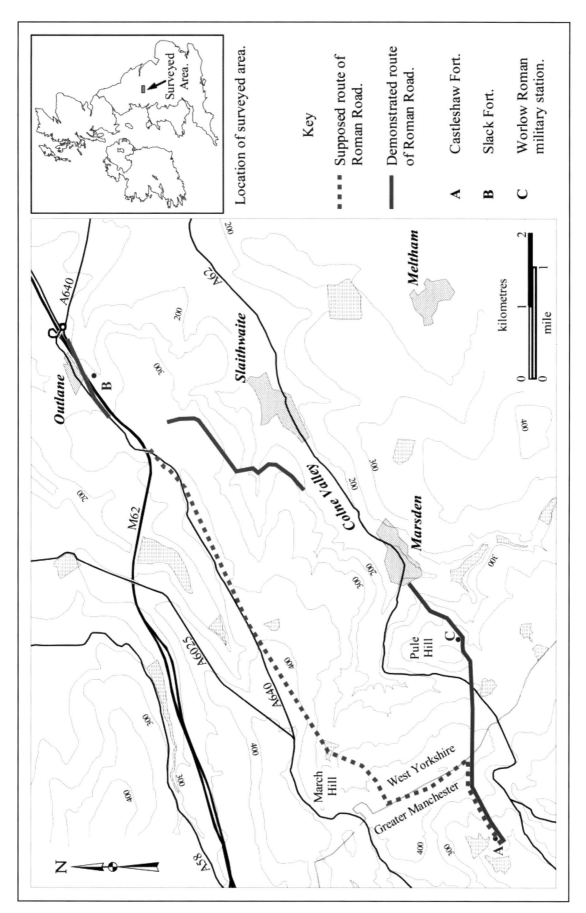

Location of surveyed area.

Key

▪▪▪▪ Supposed route of Roman Road.

—— Demonstrated route of Roman Road.

A Castleshaw Fort.

B Slack Fort.

C Worlow Roman military station.

Map 1

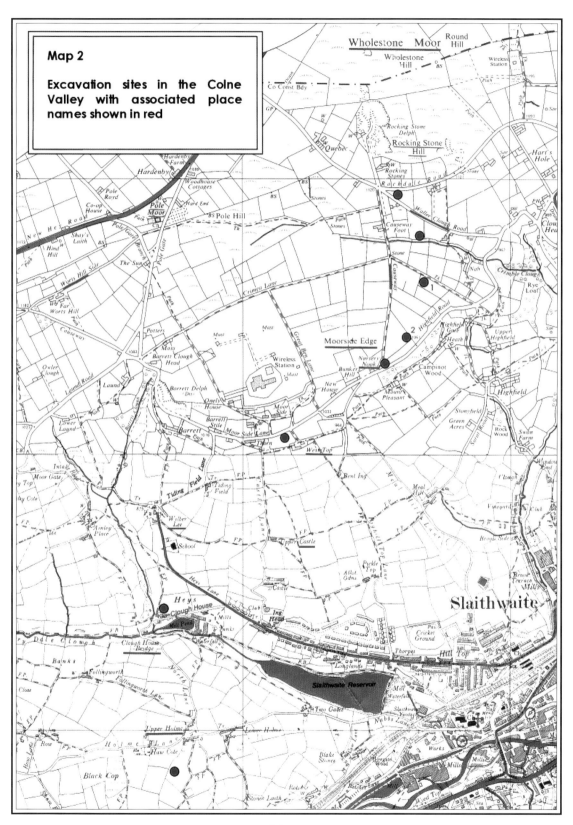

Map 2

Chapter 1

MOORSIDE EDGE 1973

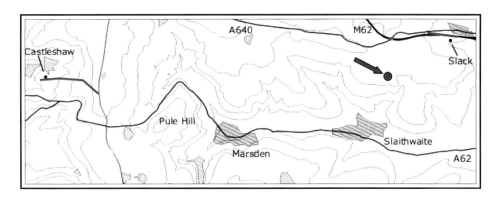

Mr. George Dransfield who farmed at Moorside Edge was a work colleague of Norman Lunn the Director of Excavation and Fieldwork of the Huddersfield Society. He was anxious to level one of his fields by removing a ridge which ran in a more or less north/south direction, but he had the good sense to seek advice before doing so. He had no wish to damage or destroy any structure of historical interest which might be hidden beneath the ground. He naturally turned to Norman who readily agreed to have a look at the field and then offer an opinion as to what should be done.

As a consequence, one September Saturday a small party of HDAS members assembled in the field which lies adjacent to the trackway leading from Highfield Road to Crimea Lane. A prominent ridge extended across the length of the field. One member of the party commented that it had been examined some years before and that the label of 'linear bank' had been attached to it *(Plate 2)*.

Plate 2 - Ridge or 'Linear Bank' emphasised by changing depth of drystone wall.

Probing was rewarded when stone was encountered about twenty five centimetres below the present ground surface and this appeared to extend for six metres or so across the feature.

This system of investigation gave every indication of the presence of a road hitherto not known to exist in this situation.

Mr. Dransfield was advised of the findings and readily agreed to suspend any work in the field until the site had been properly explored by the Society.

Excavation would only be possible at weekends as all the potential diggers had work and family commitments. Then there was the problem of cattle which would be grazing in the field, at least until the onset of winter. We would need to fence the trench to avoid damage from the hooves of inquisitive cows, and certainly to protect the animals themselves from injury. So a fence was duly constructed and transported to the site in sections. We were now happy that the trench could be kept open between weekends. Fortunately the site was readily accessible, and indeed as winter progressed it was possible to bring a Land Rover into the field which on many occasions provided very welcome shelter.

Plate 3 - Unique shot of road foundation.

Excavation commenced with a trench across the line of the apparent road material. It would be extended in due course to look for any ditches which might be anticipated and would assume some considerable length before the investigation was completed.

Road metal appeared around 25 cm or so below the ground surface, thus confirming the results obtained by the initial probing; it had an average depth of 23 cm towards the centre of the road. Much of the surface material had been spread by ploughing. There were no 'early' finds in the plough spread but pot from the Victorian era and fragments of clay pipe were much in evidence as one might anticipate in such a situation.

It became clear that the road metal consisted of graded stones; the larger flatter pieces closely packed together being used towards the base, with the smaller more gravel-like material being placed towards the surface. The ultimate foundation material consisted of slabs of sandstone, some being of considerable size. These were roughly placed to form a sort of pavement; this is clearly demonstrated in *Plate 3*. Beneath these large flat stones was a distinct layer of buried humus which represented the surface material contemporary with the time when the road was constructed. This lay on top of the natural clay of the locality. There was evidently no need to totally clear the ground before building started at this location. The road demonstrated a modest camber, there being a fall on both sides of the crown of at least 16 cm. No doubt if the road surface had been more complete and not destroyed and scattered by ploughing, the camber would have been appropriately exaggerated. There was no evidence of kerbstones in situ.

Here then at Moorside Edge we had a road some seven metres in width with associated ditches. The southern ditch was of a scooped type being three and a half metres in width and 75 cm at its maximum depth. The inner lip was three metres from the edge of the road and there was some evidence of silting. This ditch contained a number of large flat stones probably indicating road foundation material or perhaps even kerbstones together with a great deal of road metal. The northern ditch was three metres wide, 60 cm in depth and was likewise placed three metres from the edge of the road but contained a considerable amount of silt. There were no material finds in either ditch.

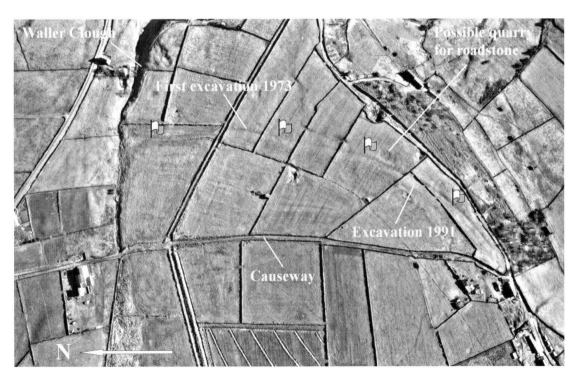

Plate 4 - Line of road and excavation sites, Moorside Edge
(Original 1971 aerial photo courtesy of English Heritage, National Monuments Record)

Situated along the line of the road and at no great distance from the southern ditch is a succession of small, shallow hollows which are evidently quarries. These are beautifully demonstrated on aerial photographs *(Plate 4)*. They almost certainly represent the sources of material obtained to augment that excavated from the ditches, then to be used as graded roadstone.

As excavation progressed, so did the onset of winter, and we had a real winter in that of 73-74 with weeks of sub zero temperatures and a modest amount of snow. As stated earlier Norman Lunn's Land Rover was a present from the Gods under these conditions, and the sight of Bon Spence suddenly appearing through the mist and snow is implanted on the memory for ever. There was only one problem for the diggers so marooned. The close proximity of the B.B.C. North Regional transmitter at Moorside Edge meant that only one station could be received on the radio. In fact people living nearby would have us believe that even their electric ovens played Radio One! In the late winter however, when the time came for filling in, the thaw arrived together with the rain. The site became a quagmire with the replaced turves more or less floating on the sodden clay.

On a much more serious note, the photography was almost a total disaster. All three cameras that were used developed faults, some in fact directly as a result of the bitterly cold weather. Only the Secretary produced any photographs at all, and most of those were out of focus.

The section drawing was also conducted under trying conditions with constant snow flurries and bad light adding to the difficulty of the numb fingers of those who took it in turn to draw. Looking back, the excavation from start to finish was something of a triumph over adversity on this exposed Pennine slope reaching 330 metres above sea level during the harsh winter months. It is the only occasion that the Society has conducted an extended excavation in the winter months.

At this time we had a length of road, but a length of road in some isolation. However from its characteristic style and robust manner of construction with a raised agger and well drained base, there could be little doubt of its Roman origin.

The Society had at this time conducted only one previous excavation on a Roman road. This had taken place some three years earlier along the line east of the Slack fort, at Lindley Moor on the north side of Lindley Moor Road. There things were rather different from what we were finding at Moorside Edge. Much of the road stone was well scattered, and the road was based on bedrock and not clay. The road widths were very similar, but of course it is not possible to be too specific here because of slippage. We would propose five and a half metres at Lindley Moor and seven metres at Moorside Edge. However, there was one feature at Lindley Moor that was not evident at Moorside Edge, and that was the presence under it of an earlier road of three metres width.

The late winter and early spring of 1974 saw the Society quietly congratulating itself on having carried out an excavation which was satisfactory in most respects under difficult circumstances; but the outcome posed more questions than it had answered. We had answered Mr. Dransfield's enquiry. Now we were presented with a short length of road apparently going nowhere. In the northerly direction the fort at Slack, two kilometres away, would seem to be the obvious objective. If this was so, the route would have to pass directly over or circumnavigate the southern aspect of Round Hill, Wholestone Moor. In the southerly direction it was agreed that it was almost certainly making for the upper Colne Valley although the purpose of this line was by no means clear.

It is interesting to review the statements made at the time by the directors Norman Lunn and Bill Crosland:-

'The Moorside Edge Road may then be part of an alternative route from Slack to Castleshaw via the Colne Valley, possibly an easier route to use in the winter. It may be part of a postulated route to Templeborough, or it may in fact connect Slack with undiscovered Villa settlements in the upper Colne Valley; although it would seem unnecessary to construct so substantial a road for such a purpose'.

Thirty years later we would discount the route to Templeborough. The winter route is still a possibility although there are many valid arguments opposed to this; and perhaps we should not overlook the possibility of a Villa in the Colne Valley as a future bonus.

Chapter 2

PULE HILL 1983

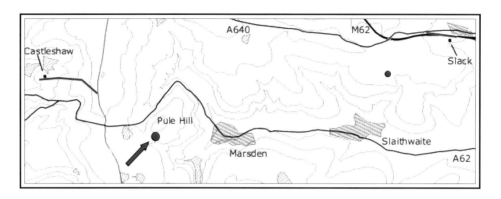

The reader may well wonder why after the discovery of a Roman road at Moorside Edge in 1973 it took a decade before another section was uncovered. In the intervening years the attention of the Society had been drawn to other sites of interest and importance. Among these both Meg Dyke and South Crosland Hall merited detailed investigation, and hence made inroads into the resources available. Here it must be borne in mind that the majority of active digging members were in full time occupations. Nevertheless field walking continued along the postulated line from Slack to Castleshaw, but perhaps very much on an occasional basis.

It was however appropriate that on one of these weekend excursions in the late summer of 1982 a group of HDAS members walking the southern slopes of Pule Hill found that probing around stone lying on the surface indicated the possibility of road material along an apparent terrace. There had been considerable moorland fires the previous summer, much of the peat being burned off, thus making it possible to identify features which had not been visible to walkers looking at this area in earlier years. As this line would seem to make a nice fit for a route between the Colne Valley and Castleshaw, it was agreed that an investigation here should be the object of excavation in the following season.

Work started in May and continued throughout the summer. Members excavated for a total of thirty days making this the most extensive dig that the Society had undertaken up to that time. What started as a simple trench grew to be very much more, as this and every subsequent trench posed further questions, some of which still remain to be answered.

Trench 1 *(See Plan 1)* along the western aspect of the terrace way proved to be something of a disappointment. Little stone remained in place; it had almost certainly been eroded by wind and rain and had possibly been used as a convenient quarry by the builders of the nearby turnpike; however it presented a fine stone lined ditch on its southern edge.

One hundred metres to the east where road had been identified the previous summer, stone was very near to the surface and it soon became apparent that our proposed Roman road here was taking the form of a Packhorse track or Causeway *(Plate 5)*. Disappointed and somewhat disheartened the diggers continued to trowel away on both sides of the Causeway thus revealing the rounded cobbles associated with a road surface. Things were beginning to look better!

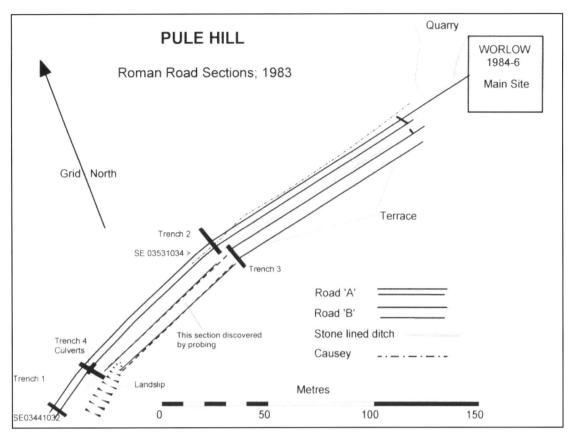

Plan 1 - Site plan of Pule Hill excavations from 1983 to 1986.

Plate 5 - Packhorse track exposed.

Trench 2 was then cut through the track; underneath the cobbles were layers of large flat stones which formed an impressive foundation *(Plate 6)*. This material extended to a depth of one metre *(Plates 8 and 9)* and gave an overall width to the road that it supported of perhaps three metres. It was a very substantial, but rather narrow road.

Plate 6 - But look what lies beneath the track.

The next trench (Trench 3) was almost an extension of Trench 2, but stepped three metres to the east. It soon became clear that another and rather different road was being uncovered (Road B). This had a width again of some three metres, but it had evidently been widened to seven metres. Buried deep in the foundation material was a large iron object, subsequently identified as a horseshoe *(Plate 7)*. Unfortunately this is the type of 'find' which may not be associated with any specific period.

Plate 7 - Horseshoe in road foundation.

Plate 8 - Section through road.

Plate 9 - They don't make them like this any more.

On the northern (uphill) aspect was a very well preserved, shallow, stone lined ditch *(Plate 10)*.

The location of Trench 3 is nicely illustrated in *Plate 11*. The photograph is taken from a position on the northern road (Road A) somewhat to the east of Trench 2. In the background is Mount Road on which the diggers' cars can be seen parked. The difficulties encountered in transporting equipment uphill over rough ground, some of it boggy, to the site need no further description.

Plate 10 - Stone lined ditch.

Trench 4, cut across Road A twenty five metres east of Trench 1, contained a well made edge consisting of large stones on its southern aspect. An interesting bonus here was the presence of a culvert which showed evidence of having been repaired *(Plate 12)*. A southerly extension included the stone lined ditch of Road B, but much of the road material had been displaced by land slip, and little remained in situ.

Two roads having been identified over a distance of 110 metres and running more or less parallel to each other, it now remained to trace them in an easterly direction towards Worlow by sight and by use of the probe. To confirm our findings, a shallow trench was excavated on Road A, 110 metres east of Trench 2, where a good road surface was revealed. Similarly, the stone lined ditch of Road B was identified in the same area.

This had been a memorable and very enjoyable season of excavation with weather and light of Mediterranean quality only spoiled one Sunday afternoon by a thunderstorm of tropical proportions.

Plate 11 - A hot day on Pule Hill.

Plate 12 - Culvert.

We did not lack for company, many interested hill walkers called in to see us. Dr. Stonehouse and the Saddleworth Society were working on a nearby flint site, and a group from Lancaster University was not far away.

Looking for one road, we had in fact found three. One was the mediaeval causeway, the other two being Roman, their provenance assured by their quality of construction and by the pieces of Romano-British pot and tile lying on the surface in erosion patches along the line at Worlow. These finds whetted the appetites as the dig drew to a close. We had a great deal to look forward to for the following season.

Chapter 3

WORLOW 1984, 1985 & 1986

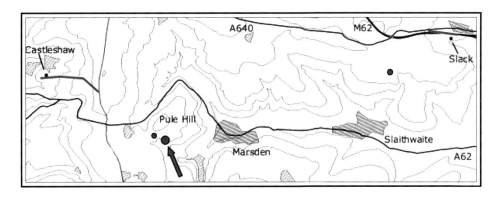

The place known as Worlow is on a spur of Pule Hill, and the area which excited our interest lies perhaps 200 metres east of trenches 2 & 3 on the site plan of the Pule Hill excavations. It is the summit of the Roman road before it makes its descent into the Colne Valley and it was in this location that fragments of Romano-British pottery were found in the summer of 1983.

The part to be investigated was a confusion of quarry and quarry spoil (*Plate 14*); and the reader may be helped to locate it if it is noted that the second flag from the right in *Plate 13* approximately marks the position of Trench 2 in the Pule Hill excavations.

The site identified for closer study was situated across the line of the road, being more or less centred on the spot where the 1983 pottery had been found. Before any excavation was started an area 35 metres square was carefully surveyed.

The work was scheduled to last for two weeks, but in fact it continued at weekends throughout the summer. Excavation at Worlow carried on for a further two seasons, making this the most extensive and perhaps the most comprehensive investigation to be undertaken by the Society.

The object of the research for this the first season and indeed for the whole project was to find further evidence of Roman occupation and to locate structures, always bearing in mind that this would be an ideal site for a signal station associated with the road. In all some six trenches were cut within the surveyed area; two others being placed just outside, purely to demonstrate the road as it approached the summit.

One trench which crossed the edge of an early quarry was particularly productive. Mixed with the quarry spoil came quantities of Romano-British material (*Plate 15*), fragments of tile and pottery, iron nails of all sizes, together with a number of sharpening stones. Some of the pottery was samian ware, and the presence of this together with beads and a bronze buckle (*Plates 16 & 17*), would seem to indicate something rather more sophisticated than a workman's site.

Plate 13 - The road to Worlow.

Plate 14 - Worlow before excavation.

Plate 15 - Pottery, nails and whetstones.

Finds from Worlow

Plate 16 - Bronze buckle.

Plate 17 - Glass melon beads.

There was no material of later provenance. The Victorian pot and clay pipe which might be anticipated in a nineteenth century quarry was just not there. It would seem very probable that we had been working in a quarry which because of the nature of its filling must be either contemporary with, or earlier than the Roman period. The material was subsequently assessed by John Walker of the Greater Manchester Archaeological Unit and pronounced to be from the first and second centuries A.D.

The diggers were fortunate to have fine weather for this first season, but it was one of those summers that was both dry and windy. Indeed as the dig progressed, dust was blown from the ever enlarging spoil heaps into the eyes and noses of the toiling Society members making work difficult on occasions.

This was also the season in which we lost our large and rather unwieldy wheelbarrow, which because of the problems of transportation was left on site overnight. We found it impossible to believe that anyone would want to steal such an object from such a remote place. But we were wrong. The digging party arrived one morning to see the wheelbarrow racing down the hill, then being loaded into a van which disappeared in a cloud of dust in the direction of Marsden.

Perhaps because of some publicity in the local newspaper, the site became prey to evening treasure hunters, who we suspected were using metal detectors. To counter this, a number of suitable iron objects were buried in strategic positions with the intention of spreading confusion among the uninvited.

The moorland sheep, always not far away, could present difficulties from time to time. Our empty trenches provided them excellent overnight accommodation which they understood to be 'en suite'. One unfortunate animal died in the vicinity; the smell eventually became so unbearable that volunteers were called for to form a burial party.

This first season at Worlow had been highly successful; a considerable quantity of Romano-British 'finds' had been unearthed, but there was no evidence at all of a structure. We felt with some confidence that the following season might treat us more kindly in this respect.

May 1985 saw the Society back on site; at weekends at first, then for two full weeks in July, after which work reverted to weekends until October.

This was a really poor summer, it rarely seemed to stop raining and it is a tribute to the considerable fortitude of the diggers that they stuck it out to the bitter end. On the positive side, there were more small finds near to the productive trenches of the previous season, but a stone structure with associated evidence of considerable burning would not be explained until the following year.

Amongst the many visitors this season were John Hedges, Director of the West Yorkshire Archaeological Unit and Phillip Mayes, Director of the Greater Manchester Unit. We were grateful to them and to their colleagues for their encouragement and advice.

The 1986 season again lasted from May until October, but this year the Society was blessed with much better weather. This is well illustrated perhaps in *Plate 18*. The Director,

Norman Lunn also had the pleasure of living more or less on site with his caravan parked nearby. This vehicle also provided welcome shelter for the diggers on the rare occasions when the weather let them down.

Plate 18 - Recording the evidence 80s' style.

Further extensive excavation in and around the stone structures located the previous year helped to identify them as rampart footings supporting a turf rampart some four to five metres in width *(Plate 19)*. Although much of the rampart had been destroyed by later quarrying, enough remained (about 20 metres) to postulate a square or rectangular structure with rounded corners.

We were assisted in obtaining a partial outline of the rampart by the use of what became known as the 'Castleshaw Kite', a remotely controlled camera suspended from a kite. This invaluable and ingenious apparatus was currently being used by Dave Start and his colleagues in their work on the Roman fort at Castleshaw. *Plate 20* which is one of the photographs taken from the kite demonstrates the curve of the outer footings of the rampart; it also shows a trench cut into the interior and two spoil heaps.

Plate 19 - Turf rampart with footings to left.

Plate 20 - A kite's eye view.

The turf rampart had been destroyed by burning, however a number of potsherds associated with it had survived *(Plate 21)*, as had an assortment of iron nails, a dolabra (a sort of Roman entrenching tool) together with a mortarium which was almost complete.

Plate 21 - Base of vessel revealed.

A great deal of effort was expended in trying to locate the ground surface in the interior of the area enclosed by the rampart. This area was of course very much reduced in size because so much had been destroyed by quarrying. To make matters worse that which remained was covered in quarry spoil, and this presented the excavators with some back breaking digging. If a signal station had been built here we hoped at least to be able to identify the footings of the supporting wooden posts, but we were to be disappointed. However, just outside the enclosed area there was an extensive and deep area of burning indicating a succession of fires in this place. One interpretation is that this could well have been associated with a signal fire.

Roman roads rarely produce finds which may be assigned with confidence to the Roman period, and this road is no exception. A horseshoe at Pule Hill, boot studs in the second excavation at Moorside Edge; these finds may or may not have a Roman origin, it is impossible to be certain. It is only at Worlow that there is a mass of Romano-British material that can be dated with some accuracy to the first and second centuries A.D., making the station and road contemporary with the forts at Slack and Castleshaw.

Worlow in reality puts the seal of authority on this military way.

Chapter 4

UPPER HOLME 1988

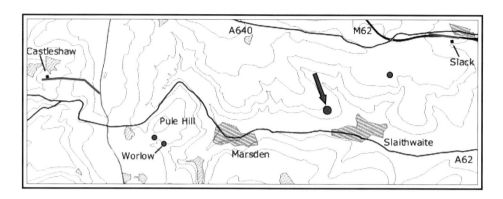

During the years which included the excavations at Pule Hill and Worlow, members were very much involved in field work in trying to link the Roman road at these sites with that identified by the Society at Moorside Edge in 1973. There was of course at the back of our minds the possibility that we could be dealing with two roads that had no direct connection with each other; however, the line at Moorside Edge gave every appearance of leading to the upper Colne Valley.

There were two possible clues to help in generally determining the line of a route. Firstly, John Warburton writing in 1720 when describing the military way east of Oldham states that, it *'passes through Saddleworth by Marsden Chapell'*. It is probable that the road crossed the Colne here at Marsden, but highly unlikely that any evidence of a crossing would remain in view of the considerable disturbance which has taken place there since mediaeval times.

Plate 22 - The 'Dyall Stone' found in Booth Bank Clough.

The second clue is the apparent Roman milestone *(Plate 22)*, known as the Dyall (or Devil) Stone, *(see enclosed CD)* in the grounds of Slaithwaite Manor House. According to the Commonplace Book of John Kaye it was discovered *'thus Roundyd'* in 1587 in Booth Bank Clough and set up in front of his house, where it can still be seen. Booth Bank lies some two kilometres northeast of Marsden on the northern slope of the Colne Valley.

There are real difficulties in looking for Roman remains on the lower slopes of the hillside on the north bank of the Colne. Here construction of first a canal and then a four track railway in the nineteenth century involved considerable earthworks with the consequent loss of any earlier features.

However, the indications were that Marsden was the place to start from in searching for a line running in a northeasterly direction towards Moorside Edge.

Approaching Ashton Binn, the path on the north side of the valley runs along a terrace way giving some indication of a possible route at this location before dropping into the steep sided Green Hill Clough. From here the road must climb quite steeply, perhaps towards Cop Hill which might be assumed to make a good sighting point. Naturally, a great deal of time was spent at Booth Bank Clough, but apart from a narrow trackway *(Plate 23)*, there was little evidence of a road here at that time. Many weekends were spent probing features both likely and unlikely in fields in and around this area, and on one Sunday afternoon we were able to identify with some certainty perhaps fifty metres of road under the turf about two hundred metres southwest of the hamlet of Upper Holme.

Plate 23 - Trackway approaching Booth Bank.

The site was in pasture land on a gently sloping plateau 235 metres in altitude. The ground rose steeply on the northern aspect, the slope away from the line being towards the Colne Valley.

A preliminary or trial excavation took place over an extended weekend in September 1987. Unfortunately the trench involved a land drain, making excavation difficult. Nevertheless it was possible to reveal enough of the feature to demonstrate the presence of a very substantial road. Further probing indicated that in an easterly direction it continued for the length of the field to be then lost under the buildings of Upper Holme. A season's excavation was then planned for the summer of 1988, bearing in mind the difficulties encountered with water on this occasion.

Plate 24 - Peeling off the layers.

*Plate 25 - Three distinct layers with water
filled ditch running left to right.*

Two weeks were set aside for the project and with a petrol-powered pump now available (*Plate 1*), it was intended to carry out a detailed examination of the method of construction. A three metre trench was adopted and fortunately sufficient members rallied round to justify the optimism of the Directors in that decision.

Road material in the form of cobbles appeared 23 cm below the modern ground surface; much of this had been dispersed by ploughing which fortunately had been of a fairly shallow nature. Below the cobbles came a distinct and discrete layer of small flat stones (*Plate 24* on the left of the trench, and *Plate 25* in the centre).

This layer was supported by three bands of equivalent material, two of which are illustrated on the left aspect of the trench in *Plate 25*. Beneath these three lines of stone came a considerable layer of shale.

Plate 26 - Central 'spine' of overlapping stones.

Plate 27 - Line of kerbstones in foreground.

This material is not natural to the location and was imported from nearby beds. The centre of the road was represented by a line of stones pitched almost vertically, but in effect overlapping each other and forming indeed a central 'spine' *(Plate 26)*. The way the stones are overlapped indicates progress from west to east (left to right on the photograph). It is thought that these stones were laid to mark the line to be taken by the road.

The trench was extended in both directions to look for ditches and those other common Roman features, kerbstones. A small ditch was located on the northern aspect, at the very edge of the road. Any kerbstones included here when the road was built would almost certainly have collapsed into the ditch in the intervening period.

On the southern (Colne Valley) end of the trench there was no ditch even though a considerable extension was made in order to look for one. We were however rewarded with a very fine line of kerbstones *(Plate 27)*.

The absence of a ditch on the southern aspect was something of a mystery, but the impressive and substantial nature of the construction together with the gentle slope towards the Colne Valley probably made a ditch here an unnecessary luxury.

In summary, at Upper Holme we had a carefully and one might say beautifully constructed road almost seven metres in width and in a perfect state of preservation. It was in fact a road of quality.

The Society was very grateful to the Director of the Greater Manchester Archaeological Unit Phillip Mayes, and to his colleagues John Walker and Dave Start for their help and advice given during the course of this work. Members were also encouraged by the considerable interest shown by the residents of Upper Holme.

Plate 28 - Precarious photography at Upper Holme, Slaithwaite.

Chapter 5

CLOUGH HOUSE BRIDGE 1989

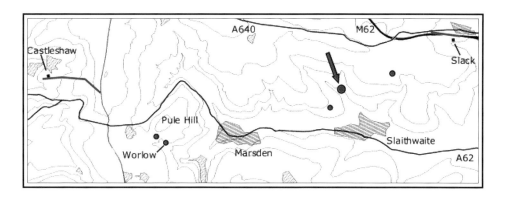

As outlined in the chapter on Upper Holme, the road leading west from the site of the Society's excavation could not be traced through the village of Upper Holme, but once it had passed here, it must at some point cross Merry Dale Clough.

Plate 29 - The road descends to Merry Dale Clough and Clough House Bridge.

There is a terrace way which originates near to the village and descends to Clough House Bridge close to and on the western side of North Lane (*Plate 29*). The evidence obtained by probing here (*Plate 30*), was conclusive of the presence of road material, with the certainty that the stream at Merry Dale Clough must be crossed in the vicinity of the present bridge leading to Clough House Lane.

Plate 30 - Looking down on Clough House Bridge in Merry Dale Clough.

Plate 31 - From Clough House Bridge to Wilberlee.

With this very much in mind, it was decided that the principal summer excavation in 1989 should take place in a field on the north side of Clough House Lane where we might anticipate the Roman road climbing up from Merry Dale Clough towards Wilberlee *(Plate 31)*.

The early summer had been very dry; when the work started it was also very hot. The diggers opted to take advantage of the low water level in the nearby stream (Barrett Clough) to have a look to see if there was any sign of an early ford here. A considerable quantity of vegetation had to be cleared away - blackberry bushes and the like - to give access to the area where the road might cross. Most sites present hazards; unpleasant smells, and ants for example. The early days at Clough House Bridge were plagued by a swarm of particularly vicious wasps, but the members soldiered on.

No rain came, and an area of small vertically pitched stones was cleared on the stream bed. These gave the appearance of forming a paving. There was also evidence of a road leading up to it, so a Roman label may be attached with modest confidence *(Plate 32)*.

Plate 32 - Possible ford at Clough House Bridge.

Now that the stream had been examined, the hot dry weather so eagerly sought but so rarely obtained by archaeologists in the Pennines became a disadvantage.

Because of the hard ground, probing in the field and up the hillside became either impossible or inconclusive, and the first week of the fortnight that had been set aside was spent on a number of test trenches which only told us where the road would not be found. It was beginning to look as though we were digging in the wrong place, but then on the Saturday night there was a thunderstorm accompanied by very heavy rain. On the Sunday morning, Brian Howcroft, joining the party on his return from holiday, took up the probe and in no time at all found sufficient stone to suggest a road surface. The rain had softened the ground enough to make the use of the probe a viable exercise once more.

Plate 33 - This is the edge of the road.   *Plate 34 - . . . and it's wide.*

A trench was then put across the road thus identified, and a very clearly defined edge appeared on its western aspect *(Plate 33)*. It soon became clear that in this location at any rate there were two roads running side by side. One was very well constructed and perhaps three and a half metres in width; the other not so well made was wider, in the region of seven metres *(Plate 34)*.

The Society subsequently borrowed a resistivity meter from the West Yorkshire Unit with the intention of tracing the paths of the two roads as they ascended the hill. Sadly, this exercise proved to be futile because of the electrical interference by the Moorside Edge radio transmitter one kilometre distant.

This investigation was concluded somewhat prematurely because the excavators ran out of time. There was a sense that there was much more to be done here and that the outcome of the resistivity survey would point us in the right direction; but this was not to be.

A particularly intriguing aspect of this locality is the proximity of an area known as Castle, a name which frequently has a Roman connection. Castle however lies slightly to the east of the postulated route; so did the more easterly of the two roads go in that direction?

This question remains to be answered.

Chapter 6

MOORSIDE EDGE 2 1991

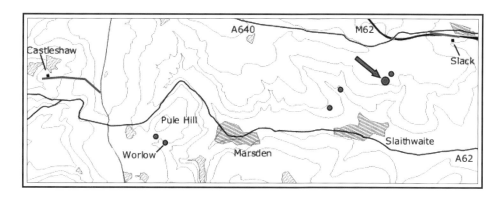

The real purpose of returning to this locality in 1991 was to obtain a photographic record of the road, along with section drawings, which would supplement and confirm the findings of 1973.

The agger running through the fields was highly visible and this was accentuated by the succession of 'humps' in the numerous drystone walls. The alignment of these was such that it pointed directly towards Pule Hill, Marsden on the skyline to the southwest (*Plate 35*).

Plate 35 - Trench across the agger.

With the approval of Mr Robert Bamforth the farmer, and landowners Dartmouth Estates, a site was chosen where the agger cut through the corner of a field (*Plate 36*).

Using the tried and trusted method of probing the ground with metal rods to determine the extent of the underlying stone it was decided that a trench 10 metres long by 2 metres would be adequate.

Plate 36 - Turf and topsoil removed.

Plate 37 - Foundation of the road.

The road surface at its centre was only 10cms below the turf; it had an overall width of 8 metres and rested on substantial foundations *(Plate 37)*. Beneath these was a continuous black layer of carbonised material which proved to be the original ground surface. The subsequent Pollen Report *(see enclosed CD)* suggested an environment of scrubland with heathers and bracken, and a small amount of tree cover.

A shallow ditch approximately 3 metres to the north afforded only token resemblance to that of the previous dig. *(See Section drawing on enclosed CD)*. Nevertheless the main purpose of this return visit had been achieved with the addition of a small bonus.

Finds on roads are not commonplace but thanks to Bill Crosland, two small blobs of rusted iron were unearthed. They came from separate locations in the lower foundations of the road. X-rays showed studs, like tiny hobnails. Is it too fanciful to imagine that they could have been lost from the footwear of a Roman soldier?

In keeping with tradition the section drawings were completed in pouring rain. Intriguingly, early maps show a standing stone adjacent to the road at SE 07651554, which Darren Bailey calculates was where the 7th Roman milestone from Castleshaw would have stood. It is no longer there.

Chapter 7

WALLER CLOUGH 1997

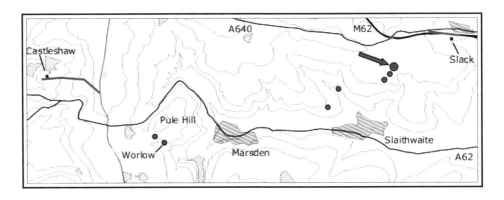

Having established beyond doubt the presence of a road of Roman appearance and characteristics it was judged that linking it to the road out of Slack would be a useful exercise.

The continuation of the road northeastwards from Moorside Edge was clearly shown on aerial photographs and was also easily visible on the ground with favourable lighting. There were, however, no obvious signs beyond Waller Clough. Wholestone Moor stood in the way. Had the surveyors chosen to go round it, west side or east side, or over the top? First of all where the road actually crossed the stream would have to be determined by probing.

Fortunately at only one point on the eastern bank of the stream was there a consistent spread of stone as opposed to the soft, effortless, deep probing experienced elsewhere along the line of the clough (*Plate 38*).

Plate 38 - From Rochdale Road looking southeastwards.

Although excavation uncovered an abundance of stone with a deep ditch to one side, this was the least convincing of all the sites we had investigated in terms of road material on top of underlying foundations which would indicate planned construction. While road material may be scattered or removed, ditches do not disappear and we certainly had these ingredients.

Plate 39 - Trenches across the road.

Plate 40 - Main trench with balk.

Plate 41 - Large stone slab with spigot hole.

The search was for a crossing point and this seemed to be it. Whether the large stone slab *(Plate 41)* played any part in the crossing of the stream is open to question.

Without further extensive excavation, this site was not going to show in which direction the road continued, and probing was inconclusive. Clearly the field to the north of the clough had been badly disturbed. The search for the route over or around Wholestone Moor would have to be made elsewhere.

Chapter 8

MILLSTONE EDGE / THIEVES CLOUGH 1999

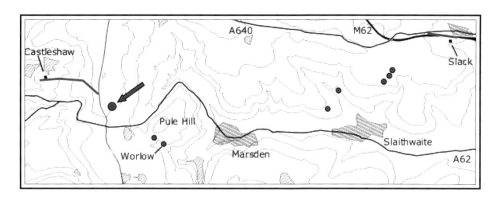

If we intended to put forward our findings as a Roman link between Castleshaw and Slack then we had to fill in more of the gaps. A move to the other end of the line seemed timely.

It was decided to test the validity of the 'Roman Road' markings on the 1 inch O.S. map of 1843. Using the 6 inch map of 1854, accurate measurements were taken from the marked field boundary walls to the dotted track which extended beyond Thieves Bridge towards the 'cutting' in the direction of Brown Rough.

Armed with 30 metre tapes and the scaled up distances a small team set out across Standedge. The vegetation proved hazardous as huge tussocks afforded unstable footing for the walkers who frequently staggered and fell full length, to disappear from sight in the long grass.

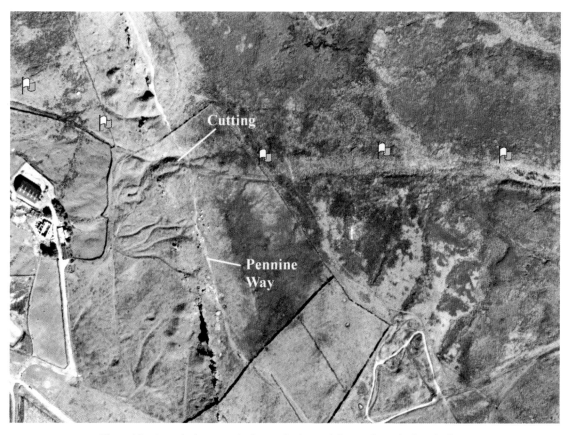

Plate 42 - Aerial photograph shows the line of the road marked with flags.

The stipulated distance of 176 metres was covered and ended not at an agger but in a wide, deep depression *(Plate 43)*. Probing was hardly necessary to determine where to open a trench as worn stones protruded from the peat and tufted grass.

Plate 43 - Cutting through the peat.

Permission had been granted by The National Trust to explore the area and, adhering to the conditions imposed by their Regional Archaeologist, Mark Newman, 4 square metres of covering vegetation was removed. The worn stones were found to be part of a compact road surface *(Plate 44)*. To the south side a ditch had been cut in the bedrock to a depth of around 40cms *(Plate 45)*.

Plate 44 - Worn road stone.

Plate 45 - Rock cut ditch.

Prior to the construction of this road it would seem that the vegetation, peat and soil were removed to expose a firm foundation of bedrock; hence the gully.

It was with regard to a spot close to here that Ammon Wrigley wrote, *'On this road about a mile from Castleshaw I exposed what I considered to be a stretch of worn pavement, but whether it is or is not Roman I am not prepared to say.'* Photographs of what is assumed to be Wrigley's excavation are in the W.H. Sikes Collection, housed in the Huddersfield Public Library.

With all the evidence we had gathered, our conclusion was that here we had a continuation of the Roman road.

A sudden drop in the level beyond the excavation site has been interpreted as road robbing: material taken by the workers for the purpose of constructing the adjacent turnpike laid out by John Metcalfe in 1759.

Plate 46 - Looking back on the road towards Castleshaw from the 'cutting'.

Plate 47 - Looking up from Gilberts towards the depression on the horizon.

The modern road depicted in *Plate 47* is the one named on the 1843 O.S. map as Roman Road. It also features in the detailed account of Metcalfe's crossing of the marshes at Pule, which is dealt with in great detail in W.B.Crump's 'Huddersfield Highways down the Ages'.

Chapter 9

PULE BENTS 2000

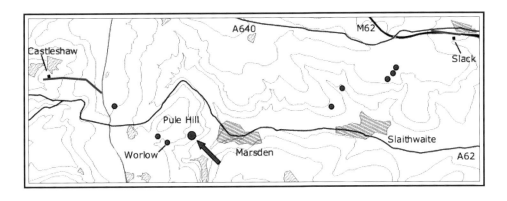

It was essential now to find proof of an exit eastwards from the Roman military station at Worlow if only to show to sceptics that this was not just a dead end link with Castleshaw. Again with the permission of the National Trust and support of Marsden Moor Estates a promising line of stones giving the impression of an agger was investigated *(Plate 48)*. The whole area is heavily disturbed by 19th century quarrying but a likely looking place to dig was agreed upon and work commenced.

Plate 48 - Downhill towards Marsden.

Appearances can be deceptive as we quickly found to our cost. The place we had chosen yielded very little that could be regarded as conclusive proof of a road. Convinced that we were on the right line we moved about 8 metres away and were rewarded with road surface material *(Plate 49)*. This material was found to cap layers of foundation stones mixed with sandy soil to an overall depth of about 30cm, sitting on a base of bedrock. The inner side was bordered by a ditch 2m wide which terminated in a low revetment wall.

Plate 49 - Road and wide ditch in foreground.

Plate 50 - Layered edge of road.

The outer edge of the road had been removed by a succession of small quarries, leaving a road width of slightly less than 5 metres.

The width of the ditch and the smoothness of some of the bedrock led Granville Clay to suggest that it had been later used by the quarrymen to transport the heavy stones on sleds down the slope to Marsden.

Plate 51 - The road from Millstone Edge to Pule Bents.
(Original photo courtesy of Greater Manchester Archaeological Unit)

Chapter 10

WEST TOP 2000

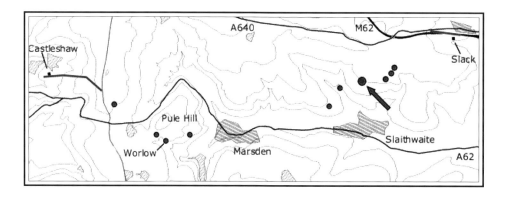

As the excavation at Pule Bents was in its closing stages, word came through that property development was taking place close to the line of the road at West Top, Slaithwaite. This was the spot where a pronounced agger had been observed as the road makes a steady climb from Wilberlee to Moorside Edge.

An urgent inspection of the site by Darren Bailey and Granville Clay confirmed that heavy earth moving equipment was being used to construct a new access road across the potential line of the Roman road to a large barn that was being converted into a detached dwelling. It was also learned that the property developer had permission to use surplus material from this activity to smooth out 'bumps' and 'hollows' in the adjoining field. It was highly likely that these irregular features were the visible remains of the agger and wide ditch of the Roman road, soon to disappear under tonnes of rubble and earth.

Plate 52 - Enigmatic arrangement of stones.

Fortunately, the property developer was both sympathetic and helpful when the situation was explained and not only allowed the Society to organise an emergency excavation but also offered the use of a mechanical digger to do all the hard work.

Part of the field, close to where the road was thought to be, had already had turf and topsoil scraped away prior to the dumping of surplus material. It was decided to open a trial trench here with a view to finding a ditch or the edge of the road. What actually emerged proved to be both puzzling and fascinating *(Plate 52)*.

What at first seemed to be a road edge with kerbstones was revealed as an isolated group of stones mostly set in vertical rows. Clearly this was not part of the road, but what was it? One plausible explanation is that we had uncovered a mason's work area where stones from nearby quarries were stacked and graded prior to building or repairing the road. Further speculation on this theory will have to be based on the photographic evidence, as the feature is now several metres below the new ground surface.

The search for the road continued with another small excavation on the apex of the visible agger. And there it was *(Plate 53)*. Closely packed, small roadstones often found as surface material on roads of Roman construction.

It only remained to find the width and depth of the road structure and any associated ditches. With time pressing the mechanical digger was brought into operation to cut a trench straight through the agger. Using the more conventional spades and trowels the road soon appeared, but it was not quite as expected *(Plate 54)*.

Plate 53 - Test pit on the agger.

Plate 54 - One road or two?

43

The ditch on the 'topside' of the road was wide and deep and still carrying water from the hillside above. There was no ditch on the lower side where the natural slope of the land would drain water away from the road. There was, however, a ditch-like depression in the centre of the road which gave rise to much speculation. Were we looking at a narrow road that was later widened or a wide road that was reduced in width using the abandoned half as repair material for the narrower road?

It should be noted here that excavations along the road have shown that where it was laid on level ground and has escaped plough damage and stone robbing, it remains in a good state of preservation. Where it was laid on sloping ground, the effects of water, weather and slippage have distorted or even destroyed the original structure. The Romans too must have had serious maintenance problems on the steep slopes of the Colne Valley.

Chapter 11

MISSING LINKS AND A LINK DISCOVERED

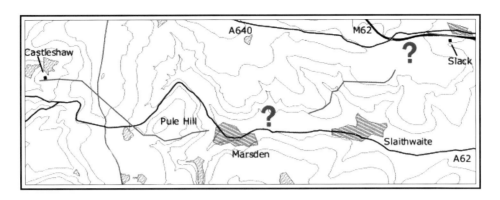

As each new site was excavated, photographed and recorded, Society members had no doubts that they had convincing evidence of a continuous Roman road linking the forts of Castleshaw and Slack; part of the military way from Chester to York. They were also aware that their discoveries could be seen as a direct challenge to the well established view, as recorded in documents, books and OS maps, that the 'official' road took a markedly different route across the high Pennines.

Reaction from sceptics to some of the early finds had varied between total disbelief and ridicule. It was for these reasons that the Society was reluctant to publish the findings until the continuous line of the road could be established beyond reasonable doubt. The search for missing sections continued, on and off, for many more years until the sensible decision was made that the work ought to be published before memories faded and records were lost.

With luck, this publication will encourage others to continue the fascinating and rewarding work of searching for the two remaining 'missing links'.

Missing Link 1
To date, no part of the road has been positively identified from the point where it starts to descend into Marsden, until it reappears in spectacular fashion on the plateau at Upper Holme, Slaithwaite. To help the search it is useful to imagine what the Colne Valley was like when the Romans first surveyed it and what factors might have determined the route between these points.

The valley bottom is likely to have been wooded, with a river fed by many moorland streams and therefore subject to periodic flooding; not a suitable place for a road. Yet the river had to be crossed at some point to get to Slack. Would it be best to proceed along the northern flank of the valley or the southern? On both sides there are ravine-like cloughs that would have to be avoided by going for higher ground or building closer to the river in potentially boggy ground.

Evidence from other sites in Britain suggests that the road would head straight for the river from higher ground, cross a shallow ford and head for high ground on the other side, clear of the flood level. However, this scenario would not work too well in the Marsden area because of the aforementioned cloughs. On the north side of the valley, a road climbing steeply out of the valley bottom would have to come back down again as it headed in a northwesterly direction, or otherwise go on to the open moorland, which the surveyors were seeking to avoid. If the road does cross the valley bottom at Marsden and continue on the north side of the River Colne, it might well take the gentle slope of Warehouse Hill and follow roughly the line of Marsden Lane, which is also the route of the ancient packhorse way from Marsden to the Calder Valley. Is it a coincidence that a trackway or packhorse way also follows the Roman road over Pule Hill?

Anyone trying to visualise the terrain in this part of the Colne Valley in Roman times has to discount all the substantial earthworks and structures associated with the canal and railway. Roads and tracks were buried or diverted and any hope of finding a direct line for the Roman road in this badly disturbed area must be abandoned. But, on the north side of the railway things are different. If the road is here then traces of it are waiting to be found. As the valley widens, the Roman surveyors could take the road on a steady incline across a small clough at Booth Bank (where the Roman milestone was found) and on to the plateau at Upper Holme, before turning in the direction of Slack (*Plate 55*).

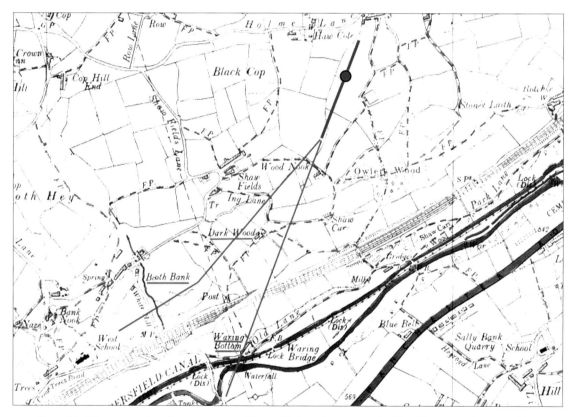

Plate 55 - Known road and excavation at Upper Holme shown in red. Possible routes shown in blue.

Another theory that had to be tested, and which led to a spectacular excavation, came from the notion that the road builders did not cross the River Colne at Marsden but followed a line along the southern side of the valley before crossing at a point much nearer to Upper Holme. This would have meant fording the Wessenden Brook, then quickly finding higher ground by following the (very straight looking) line of the present day Meltham Road which is itself part of the first turnpike road to cross this part of the Pennines.

Hopes rose when Darren Bailey donned his wet-suit and found a 'ford like' stone structure in the bed of the Wessenden Brook beneath a textile mill that stood on the line of the theoretical road. A similar structure of tightly packed vertical stones was also found in the River Colne at Waring Bottom, again on the line of the theoretical road. But hopes began to fade when probing with metal rods along the postulated line of the road failed to find any sign of a continuous stone structure. It was known that much Roman stonework was robbed during later ground clearances and the construction of drystone field walls, but when all other evidence has gone it should still be possible to find the ditches associated with a typical Roman road.

Plate 56 - The 75m Dark Wood trench.

In a brave effort to keep the theory alive, Darren Bailey decided to search for ditches by excavating a continuous trench across a field below Dark Wood farm where the road was thought to be *(Plate 56)*. His monumental 75m long trench broke all Society records for a single handed dig - but the ditches were nowhere to be found.

As for the 'stone built fords'; subsequent investigation showed that the River Colne and many fast flowing streams in the valley have been revetted and stone lined in places where they are vulnerable to scouring and erosion at times of heavy rainfall. This not only strengthens the water channel but also helps to protect the foundations of bridges, walls and riverside buildings.

Such disappointments as this are invariably the cue for one of the Society's optimists to declare - 'Well, at least, we've proved a negative!'

But not all was negative; the then occupants of Dark Wood farm took a keen interest in the search for Roman remains and subsequently unearthed a single fragment of Roman pottery in their garden *(Plate 57)*. It was identified by the West Yorkshire Archaeology Advisory Service as probably Rossington Bridge black-burnished ware from South Yorkshire, which had limited distribution in northern Britain during the 2nd century AD. Following this significant find, the search for the 'missing link' has continued in a very promising area of land immediately to the north of the farm house.

Plate 57 - Roman pottery find at Dark Wood.

Plate 58 - Emergency dig at Nursery Nook, Moorside Edge.

Missing Link 2

From Upper Holme the road has been located by probing and excavation as it crosses the steep sided Merry Dale Clough at Clough House Bridge, then climbs out of the Colne Valley in a northerly direction to get to Slack (Map 2). A pleasing addition to this accumulated evidence came in early 2004 when the ever watchful Darren Bailey noticed that a substantial field wall was being rebuilt at Nursery Nook on Moorside Edge. It appeared to be exactly on the line where the road was thought to be. Sure enough, as the foundations for the new wall were being dug (and extended by Darren in an emergency dig) there were the stone layers of the southern edge of road, with a buried humus layer beneath and evidence of a ditch *(Plate 58)*.

Those following the route of the road today might wonder what persuaded the Roman surveyors to take such a seemingly indirect line along Moorside Edge before swinging back in the direction of Rocking Stone Hill and the final obstacle, Wholestone Moor.

Again, imagination is required. What was the terrain like for the pioneer road builders? Until very recently, when extensive land drains were laid, the flat moorland from Moorside Edge to Pole Moor was extremely wet and marshy, even in summer. Much easier then to follow the rocky outcrop that runs along the edge of the moor which would also help to supply the copious amounts of stone needed for road construction and repair.

Another factor to be considered is that Roman military roads built in hilly areas tend to follow contours where the marching legions had a clear view of the land around them. This was not only to guard against surprise attack, but also to openly display the might of Rome to those in the conquered territories. The road along Moorside Edge and indeed much of the road from Castleshaw to Slack fits this description perfectly.

Having arrived back at the site of the original 1973 excavation, Society members had still to find the link from there to Slack. Did it go to the east or west of Wholestone Moor or straight over the top? The 1997 dig had found the crossing of the stream at Waller Clough but extensive probing, field walking and study of aerial photos produced no clue as to where the road went from there.

The reader might wonder why Geophysical Prospection, so ably demonstrated by television archaeologists, was not brought into use. The answer is that it was, and as far back as 1988 when new equipment was being developed by Arnold Aspinall at the University of Bradford. This was followed by Emma Wood (a Society member who also worked on TV's 'Time Team') using the most up-to-date equipment in 2004.

There were two major reasons why this method produced only patchy results. Early equipment was badly affected by the many radio transmitters situated in this part of the Pennines, and even the better shielded later equipment has difficulty in differentiating between a stone road and the stony ground on which it is built!

With motorway landscaping to the west of Wholestone Moor and extensive quarrying on top, it was feared that the link might never be found and the sceptics might never be silenced. But then a new factor appeared on the scene. An influx of new Society members, fired up by tales of the long search for the road, brought a new enthusiasm to the search. With some of the 'veterans' pointing out likely places on the slope of Rocking Stone Hill, a series of trial excavations took place that, at first, produced plenty of spoil heaps and much stone, but nothing that looked like a Roman road.

Then in late 2007, as this book was almost complete, permission was given by the landowner to sink a test pit in a small triangular shaped field between Waller Clough Road and Rochdale Road. Probing indicated a spread of stone about 7m wide, matching that of a typical Roman road *(Plate 59)*. The test pit, positioned at the edge of this spread, came straight down on what had eluded the Society for so long - a row of large, carefully placed kerbstones. The subsequent two day dig, in freezing temperatures, revealed the full width of the surviving foundation layer of the road and the two ditches *(Plate 60)*.

Plate 59 - Probing detects the width and direction of the missing road.

Plate 60 - Surviving foundation layer and ditches on the slope of Rocking Stone Hill.

Plate 61 - The 'Missing Link' detectives, Pat Woods, Steven Wroe, Warren Bower, Chris O'Prey, Nick Brook, Darren Bailey, Neil Marsay, Gillian Hoyle & Frances Hobart.

Plate 62 - Rocking Stone Hill excavation shows the road passing to the west of Wholestone Moor.

The key question has been answered; the road passes round the western slope of Wholestone Moor in the direction of Slack fort. The original ambition of the Society to prove a continuous line of the road from Castleshaw to Slack has been demonstrated beyond reasonable doubt.

Efforts can now be concentrated on filling in more of the gaps and answering some of the remaining questions.

Where does the road cross the River Colne?
What line does it take to get to Upper Holme?
Why do we seem to have two roads at both Clough House Bridge and West Top?
Was there a diversion from these two places to the area intriguingly named 'Castle'?
Can the road still be found on the western slopes of Wholestone Moor?
Where does it meet the known stretch of road that passes Slack fort?
For how long was the road used as a major transpennine route?

There is still much to do!

BIBLIOGRAPHY AND ASSOCIATED READING

Barber F., 1869-70, 'Excavations at Slack'. *Yorkshire Archaeological Journal*, Vol.I.

Booth K., 2001, *Roman Saddleworth.* Saddleworth Archaeological Trust.

Clay G., McDonnell G., Spence B. & Vernon R., 2006, *The Iron Makers of Myers Wood.* (revised 2nd edn.), HDAS.

Crosland W.E., 1972, 'A Roman Road at Lindley Moor'. *HDAS Brigantian* Vol.1.

Crump W.B., 1949, *Huddersfield Highways Down The Ages.* The Tolson Memorial Museum, Huddersfield.

Dodd P.W. & Woodward A.M., 1922, 'Excavations at Slack 1913-1915'. *Yorkshire Archaeological Journal*, Vol. XXVI.

Eastwood J., 1959, 'The Greetland Altar'. *HDAS Bulletin* No.4.

Freeman M., 1991, *Slaithwaite - A Saunter round the Centre.* The Colne Valley Society.

Haigh D., 1982, *A Survey of Roman Road Margary 712 Through The Oldham Area.* Bradford Grammar School Archaeological Society and The 712 Group.

Haigh Rev.D.H., 1877, 'Where was Cambodunum?' *Yorkshire Archaeological Journal*, Vol.IV.

Hallam A., 1965, 'The Roman Tilery in Grimscar Wood'. *HDAS Bulletin* No. 16.

Hartley B.R. and Fitts R.L., 1998, *The Brigantes.* Alan Sutton.

Holder P.A., 1982, *The Roman Army in Britain.* Batsford.

Hunter J.K.T., Manby T.G., and Spaul J.E.H., 1971, 'Recent excavations at the Slack Roman fort near Huddersfield'. *Yorkshire Archaeological Journal* Vol.42

Lunn N., 1963, 'A preliminary report on the 1963 excavations at Hagg Wood'. *HDAS Bulletin* No. 13.

Lunn N., 2002, *Slate Pits Wood, Meltham.* HDAS.

Margary I.D., 1967, *Roman Roads in Britain.* London.

Purdy J.G. and Manby T.G., 1973, 'Excavations at the Roman Tilery at Grimescar, Huddersfield, 1964'. *Yorkshire Archaeological Journal*, Vol.45.

Redmonds G., 1982, *The Heirs of Woodsome.* Huddersfield.

Richmond I.A., 1925, *Huddersfield in Roman Times.* Tolson Memorial Museum Publications.

Toomey J.P., 1967, 'The Romans in the Pennines - I'. *HDAS Bulletin* No. 20.

Toomey J.P., 1967, 'The Romans in the Pennines - II'. *HDAS Bulletin* No. 21.

Toomey J.P., 1976, 'An Iron Age enclosure at Oldfield Hill, Meltham'. Special report, *HDAS Brigantian.*

Toomey J.P., 1982, 'An inner ditch enclosure at Royd Edge, Meltham'. *HDAS Brigantian* Vol. 5.

Walker J.K., 1865, 'On the Roman Hypocaust discovered at Slack'. A paper read to the *Huddersfield Archaeological and Topographical Association.*

Walker J.S.F., (ed), 1986, *Roman Manchester - A Frontier Settlement.* The Archaeology of Greater Manchester, Vol.3. Greater Manchester Archaeological Unit.

Walker J.S.F., (ed), 1989, *Castleshaw - The Archaeology of a Roman Fortlet.* The Archaeology of Greater Manchester, Vol.4. GMAU.

Warburton J., 1720, Lansdowne MSS, British Museum.

Whitehead L.B., 1942, *Bygone Marsden.* Percy Brothers Ltd. Hotspur Press.

Wrigley A., 1912, *Songs of a Moorland Parish.*

INDEX

Entries in **bold** indicate pages on which illustrations and their captions occur.

People

NOTES